SCI-FI
OR
STEM?™

REVIVING EXTINCT SPECIES

Rosen
YA
New York

CAROL HAND

Published in 2019 by The Rosen Publishing Group, Inc.
29 East 21st Street, New York, NY 10010

Copyright © 2019 by The Rosen Publishing Group, Inc.

First Edition

Library of Congress Cataloging-in-Publication Data

Names: Hand, Carol, 1945– author.
Title: Reviving extinct species / Carol Hand.
Description: New York: Rosen Publishing, 2019. | Series: Sci-Fi or STEM? | Audience: Grades 7–12. | Includes bibliographical references and index.
Identifiers: LCCN 2017050795| ISBN 9781508180401 (library bound) | ISBN 9781508180418 (pbk.)
Subjects: LCSH: Extinct animals—Cloning—Juvenile literature. | Extinct animals—Genetics—Juvenile literature. | Rare animals—Cloning—Moral and ethical aspects—Juvenile literature.
Classification: LCC QL88 .H36 2019 | DDC 591.68—dc23
LC record available at https://lccn.loc.gov/2017050795

Manufactured in the United States of America

CONTENTS

Billionaire John Hammond had a dream and nothing was going to stop him from achieving it. Hammond wanted to develop a new theme park—something the modern world had never seen. He would clone long-extinct dinosaurs and place them on an island off Costa Rica. He would call it Jurassic Park. There would be 6-foot (1.8-meter) predators called velociraptors and gigantic 80-foot (24.4-m) *Apatosaurus*, the gentle vegetarians. There would be *Stegosaurus* and *Tricerotops*, figures from childhood play brought to life. And, of course, there would be *Tyrannosaurus rex*, the terrifying, deadly tyrant lizard. In Jurassic Park, Hammond would keep these regenerated creatures in large (but secure) habitat areas. They would be separated, as in a zoo, so the park's attractions could not eat one another. Visitors would take safarilike tours in computer-controlled jeeps. In fact, Jurassic Park would be almost entirely computer controlled, with very few human employees. What could possibly go wrong?

Hammond carried out his project in secret, outside the United States. This helped him avoid possible competitors and what he considered unnecessary regulations. But, before the park opened, his lawyers brought scientists to the island to sign off on its safety, just

in case. Allen Grant, a paleontologist (a scientist who studies fossils) and dinosaur expert, and Ellie Sattler, a paleobotanist (extinct plant expert), had studied the bones of these extinct animals. They were thrilled to see the live animals walking around but also horrified by the dangers. Ian Malcolm, a mathematician, had predicted disaster from the beginning, based on chaos theory. "Hammond's project," Malcolm said, "is another apparently simple system—animals within a zoo environment—that will eventually show unpredictable behavior." But Hammond was so confident of his park's safety that he even brought his two young grandchildren on the tour.

Almost immediately, things began to go wrong. Dennis Nedry, the disgruntled designer of the park's computer system, conspired with Hammond's chief competitor to steal dinosaur embryos. The theft required Nedry to turn off the entire computer system, including electric fences and other security features. Meanwhile, a tropical storm blew in. Soon, dinosaurs were roaming free over the island, stalking and killing people. The park's structures, presumed indestructible, were ripped to shreds. Just as Dr. Malcolm had predicted, chaos reigned in Jurassic Park. The scientists (and grandchildren) survived, but barely.

Genetic engineering alters organisms by manipulating their DNA. In de-extinction, scientists try to reconstruct extinct species by cloning them from fossil DNA or other preserved sources. When Michael Crichton wrote *Jurassic Park* in 1990, genetic engineering was a young science. Everyone saw its promise; few considered its possible misuses, and most assumed it could be controlled. For example, in Crichton's book, the geneticists did not think live animals would not necessarily behave as their makers intended. Certainly, no one expected them to be intelligent. Nedry turned off the computer and then was killed by dinosaurs, leaving no one who completely understood the computer system. Then, a storm appeared.

Visitors to Jurassic Park suffered the consequences when developers failed to anticipate the park's dangers. One consequence was being hunted by dinosaurs, such as this *Tyrannosaurus rex*.

All these factors were unpredictable, but they all happened, as such things do in complex systems.

Crichton used science fiction to sound an alarm about the dangers of unpredictable factors in new science and technology, whether genetic engineering or computerization. He described how unpredictability leads to chaos in any complex system. Finally, he questioned the ethics of implementing science and technology no one understands. In short, he said, reviving extinct species sounds like a great idea. But is it really?

CHAPTER 1

THE PROMISE OF DE-EXTINCTION

Celia was the last bucardo on Earth. The bucardo, or Pyrenean ibex, was a species of wild goat native to the Pyrenees Mountains. In a 2013 *National Geographic* article, Carl Zimmer told Celia's story. When Celia was discovered in 1999, wildlife veterinarian Alberto Fernández-Arias fitted her with a radio collar. Nine months later, in January 2000, she was crushed to death by a falling tree, and her species was officially extinct. However, a team of French and Spanish scientists preserved some of her cells and tried to bring Celia (and thus her species) back to life. The scientists removed the DNA from fifty-seven goat eggs and injected nuclei from Celia's cells into them. They implanted the eggs into surrogate mother goats. Only seven goats got pregnant. Only one carried her Celia clone to term. The baby was born on July 30, 2003, but survived only ten minutes. One of her lungs had grown a huge extra lobe, which was solid, like a liver. She could not have been saved.

The Pyrenean ibex, or bucardo, went extinct in 2000. Here, one of the last remaining pairs poses on rocks in the mountains of Andalucia, Spain.

Cloning Celia was the first attempt at recovering an extinct species—a process called de-extinction, resurrection biology, or species revivalism. Until the twenty-first century, extinction was considered final—the species was gone from Earth forever. But scientists began to wonder if they could re-create at least some extinct species from DNA present in fossils or in recently deceased animals, such as Celia. Michael Crichton's *Jurassic Park* fueled the notion, but until today, the science of biotechnology has lacked the precision tools to re-create successfully any species. Fernández-Arias, head of Spain's Aragon Hunting, Fishing and

Thriller writer James Rollins, shown here, delved into some of the darker possibilities of reviving extinct and endangered species in his 2014 novel, *The 6th Extinction*.

Wetlands Department, had been waiting for science to catch up with science fiction. According to Zimmer, in 2013, Fernández-Arias said, "We are at that moment."

FICTIONAL ATTEMPTS AT DE-EXTINCTION AND CLONING

Except for Michael Crichton, few science fiction (sci-fi) authors have tackled the concept of animal de-extinction. The most notable is probably James Rollins, whose 2014 scientific thriller *The 6th Extinction* pits two groups of geneticists against each other. A group of preservationists want to stem the tide of rapid extinction by saving existing species. This group uses genetic engineering techniques both to revive already extinct species and to increase survival by

SCI-FI SOURCES

Jurassic Park by Michael Crichton tells the story of people who thought they could control nature and found they could not. The folly of their thought process is narrated by mathematician Dr. Ian Malcolm, an expert in chaos theory. "Chaos theory," according to Malcolm, "says that you can never predict certain phenomena ... You're going to engineer a bunch of prehistoric animals and set them on an island ... A lovely dream ... But it won't go as planned. It is inherently unpredictable, just as the weather is." Malcolm explains why the cloned dinosaurs cannot be controlled. He says, "The history of evolution is that life escapes all barriers. Life breaks free. Life expands to new territories. Painfully, perhaps even dangerously. But life finds a way."

The story's events justify Malcolm's predictions. The dinosaurs do, indeed, find a way to reproduce, though their creators insisted they could not. They break free of their barriers at the first opportunity and expand into new territory. Malcolm concludes, "Scientists are actually preoccupied with accomplishment. So they are focused on whether they can do something. They never stop to ask if they *should* do something."

engineering changes in existing species. The other group assumes human actions have already doomed existing species. They use genetic engineering to design much more aggressive, vicious species to take over Earth.

Most related books, movies, and TV shows involve human cloning. Cloning is the process of making an exact replica of a biological unit (a piece of DNA, a cell, or an organism). The units are identical if their DNA is identical. The Human Cloning Foundation recommended the novel *The Genesis Code* (1998) by John Chase. This book unlocks a mystery surrounding a fertility clinic's use of DNA and genetic engineering and considers the ethics surrounding the use of these techniques. *The Boys from Brazil* (1976), by Ira Levin, was made into a movie in 1978. In the novel, Nazi scientist Dr. Josef Mengele escaped to Brazil after World War II and created a number of clones of Adolf Hitler. By adopting them into homes similar to Hitler's childhood home, Mengele hoped to create another Hitler.

Some novels are more positive. Kate Wilhelm's sci-fi novel, *Where Late the Sweet Birds Sang* (1976), describes a community trying to preserve itself by cloning after a holocaust has made humans sterile. *The Bones of Time* (1996), by Kathleen Ann Goonan, uses cloning to re-create genius and benefit humankind. David Brin creates a complex society in which clones play an important role in *Glory Season* (1993). In *Embryo* (1999), Charles Wilson deals with the creation of artificial wombs, often considered the next logical step after cloning. The James Rollins thriller *Bone Labyrinth* (2015) considers possible interbreeding between early humans and Neanderthals. Resulting genetic changes led to "hybrid vigor" and a spike in human intelligence.

In 2016, the website Futurism.media picked "the best clone movies." *The Island* (2005) deals with cloning for organ harvesting and surrogate motherhood. In *Blade Runner* (1982), clones are not considered human, and those living among humans are hunted down and killed. In *The 6th Day,* cloning occurs routinely but human cloning is forbidden. *Star Wars Episode II: Attack of the Clones* (2002) features a massive clone army. In *Splice* (2009), genetic engineers splice human and animal DNA

In the sci-fi television series *Orphan Black* (2013–2017), actress Tatiana Maslany plays several clone sisters, who meet accidentally and then become ensnared in unraveling the conspiracy of their origins.

to create an organism for medical testing. *Multiplicity* (1996) considers how a nonscientist would react to having many copies of himself, each with his own personality.

In the television series *Orphan Black* (2013–2017), the lead character discovers that she is part of a sinister cloning project and has many clone sisters. The clones work together to close the project and find a cure for the disease that is killing the clones, all while figuring out how they can live normal lives.

These media treatments of cloning consider many of its implications. Their emphasis is on story, not science. However, they open readers' or viewers' minds to the new types of genetic engineering techniques that have become available. They help people imagine how these technologies might make the future very different from the past and present.

WHY DE-EXTINCTION?

Genetic engineering is already valuable for human life. Its techniques produce medicines such as insulin and improved agricultural products. A related new field, human gene therapy (HGT), may soon cure genetic disorders. The greatest promise may be therapeutic cloning, in which DNA is used to produce an embryonic clone whose cells could grow replacement organs or neurons to replace those damaged by Alzheimer's disease or other disorders. But how can these techniques benefit other animals?

Extinction in the late twentieth century and early twenty-first has been occurring at up to ten thousand times the normal (background) rate of one to five species per year. Biologists are extremely worried about this loss in Earth's biodiversity. Most are committed to slowing the rate of species loss through conservation techniques. But, for recently extinct species, some are also considering the possibility of de-extinction. Their reasons differ. Some feel obligated to re-create species destroyed by human recklessness. Others think de-extinction will inspire the public and create greater support for species preservation. Others want to learn about past life by recreating it. They can learn much more from studying the behavior and biology of living organisms than by studying fossils.

As Crichton pointed out in the introduction to *Jurassic Park*, genetic engineering differs from previous scientific revolutions. It was conducted in thousands of laboratories around the world, rather than confined to a single laboratory. It was immediately commercialized, and most genetic engineers had a single goal—to get very rich. The motivation behind much of their research was frivolous, not scientific. Crichton gave examples such as engineering pale trout for easy visibility in streams and injectable scent cells

THE SIXTH EXTINCTION

In the last five hundred million years of life on Earth, there have been five mass extinctions. In each case, waves of species died off relatively rapidly (in geological time), eliminating most of Earth's species. Each time, the die-off was followed by a build-up of species, which evolved to fill the many vacated ecological niches. The last mass extinction was the loss of the dinosaurs sixty-five million years ago. Extinctions are a natural phenomenon. They constantly occur at a background rate of perhaps one to five species per year, with an occasional mass extinction. But in the twenty-first century, extinctions are occurring much more rapidly. Dozens of species go extinct every day. By mid-century, Earth could lose one-third to one-half of its entire species.

Past mass extinctions resulted from natural events, such as asteroid strikes, massive volcanic eruptions, or climatic changes. This century's sixth extinction is human caused, by factors such as destruction of habitat, introduction of exotic species, and global climate change. Of the threatened species, 99 percent are being threatened by people. Scientists know that a thousand species have gone extinct in the past five hundred years. Because of the destruction of natural ecosystems, thousands of others have disappeared before they could even be described.

mimicking a favorite perfume. Finally, no one was controlling the research. There were no federal laws or regulations or even scientific watchdogs. But the revolution is maturing. Scientists are beginning to think beyond the fascination of genetic engineering to its more serious implications.

CHAPTER 2

THE PROCESS OF DE-EXTINCTION

s de-extinction of species really possible? What factors are necessary for it to occur? True de-extinction requires DNA from the extinct animal. Recovering DNA depends on several things, including how long the animal has been extinct. For dinosaurs from sixty-five million years ago, there is no chance—DNA does not survive that long. How about the dodo, a flightless bird wiped out 400 years ago by sailors landing on its home island of Mauritius? Recovering the dodo is also unlikely. DNA is not preserved on hot, tropical islands. Much more possible is the woolly mammoth. Although they went extinct 3,700 years ago, mammoths lived in the frozen north. Cold is a much better preserver of DNA than tropical heat.

But finding complete genomes, or sets of DNA, from any extinct animal is highly doubtful. At best, there will be fragments. Scientists might (as the geneticists in *Jurassic Park* did) fill in missing fragments with DNA from the extinct animal's closest relative (a species of pigeon in the case of dodos). Then,

The dodo was discovered on Mauritius in 1598. Sailors wiped it out by 1662. No photos and few paintings exist of actual dodos, but they probably looked similar to the pair depicted here.

according to Carl Zimmer in *National Geographic*, they might reverse engineer, or work backward from the genome of, the pigeon species to produce dodos—or something similar to dodos.

THREE PATHS TO DE-EXTINCTION

In March 2013, *National Geographic* devoted an entire issue to the topic of de-extinction. In this issue, author Brian Switek outlined several possible methods for de-extincting a species, using the woolly mammoth as an example. Switek cautions, however, that de-extinction is more a marketing gimmick than a real possibility. Nothing will bring back the exact animal. Switek says, "Instead of truly restoring species just as they were, we would be creating the woolly mammoth … assembled from tattered DNA remnants and a base stock of their closest living relatives." Also, reconstructed animals would be returned to different habitats than those the species once lived in. Three possible methods have been suggested for bringing at least a close likeness of extinct species back to life.

CLONING FROM AN INTACT CELL

The first method, cloning, receives the most publicity but is also the least likely. True cloning requires a complete genome obtained from a living organism. By definition, this procedure cannot happen with de-extinction. In the case of woolly mammoths, some complete

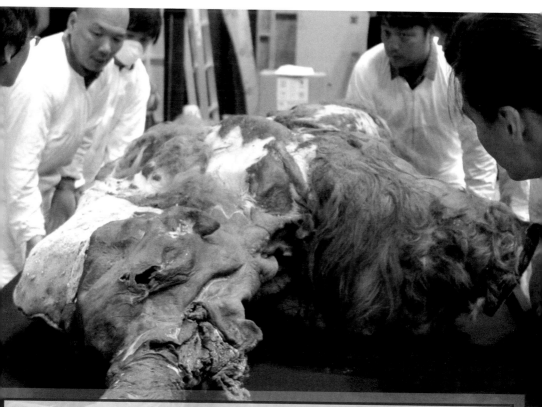

Yuka is a thirty-nine-thousand-year-old female baby mammoth recovered from frozen Siberian permafrost. Frozen specimens such as Yuka have some remaining soft tissue that can provide DNA.

genomes have been obtained from frozen carcasses recovered in the Arctic. To undertake this type of cloning, the nucleus from a frozen cell would be recovered. The nucleus from the cell of an elephant egg would be removed and replaced with the mammoth nucleus. This cell would be electrically stimulated to begin dividing. Then, it would be implanted in an elephant's uterus, where it would grow to term. The elephant would give birth to a baby mammoth. This process was used successfully to clone Dolly the sheep at Scotland's Roslin Institute in 1996.

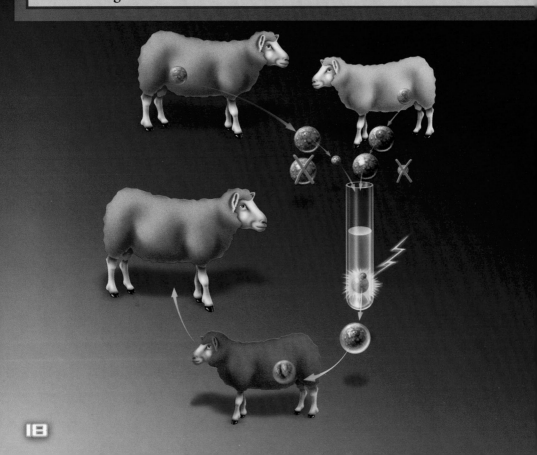

Scientists implanted a cell nucleus from one sheep into an empty cell that was then transplanted into a second sheep. Dolly (the resulting clone) had DNA from the original nucleus.

Cloning is possible only if the DNA in recovered mammoth cells is perfect; that is, if it contains all the mammoth's DNA with no missing or partial segments. Otherwise, another method must be used. For example, missing segments of mammoth DNA could be replaced by elephant DNA.

PARTHENOGENESIS: NATURAL CLONING

Parthenogenesis is asexual reproduction in which an egg cell develops into a new individual without being fertilized. Some insects, reptiles, and fish reproduce in this way. Most can also reproduce sexually. They undergo parthenogenesis when environmental conditions are not favorable, for example, when mates are scarce. This keeps the species going but decreases genetic variation. Because the offspring of parthenogenesis are identical to their mothers, this type of reproduction is genetically equivalent to cloning. But cloning is artificial, requiring the egg to be fertilized outside the body and surgically implanted.

New Mexico whiptail lizards are hybrids of the little striped whiptail and the tiger whiptail. Hybrid males do not survive, but the species continues because females reproduce parthenogenetically. It is one of very few all-female species. The Komodo dragon can also reproduce parthenogenetically. This circumstance happened in two zoos in the United Kingdom in 2006. Two Komodo dragons each laid a clutch of eggs that produced babies identical to their mothers. The dragons had not been in recent contact with males.

IN VITRO FERTILIZATION

In in vitro fertilization, an egg is fertilized outside the body and then implanted into a female's uterus. A sperm cell obtained from a frozen mammoth could be used to fertilize an elephant egg cell. The fertilized egg would be implanted into the elephant's uterus and carried to term. The elephant would deliver a hybrid elephant-mammoth. When the hybrid reached reproductive age, it would go through the same process of fertilization, again using frozen mammoth sperm cells. This technique would continue for several generations. In this type of hybridization, known as backcrossing, a hybrid is crossed with one of its parents (in this case, the mammoth father). As the process is repeated over several generations, each generation will have more mammoth genes and fewer elephant genes. Eventually, it will be considered a mammoth.

ENGINEERING FROM A SEQUENCED GENOME

In 2015, according to Pallab Gnosh of BBC News, scientists completed sequencing the mammoth genome. That is, they described the order of all bases, or building blocks, in the mammoth's DNA. An international group of scientists led by Dr. Love Dalén at the Swedish Museum of Natural History completed the study. It brings scientists one step closer to mammoth de-extinction.

Beginning with the mammoth's sequenced genetic code, scientists can take two paths. First, they can use genetic engineering techniques to build long sequences of mammoth DNA, organize them into chromosomes, and enclose them in an artificial nuclear membrane. Then, they would replace the nucleus from an elephant egg cell with the artificial mammoth nucleus. They would stimulate

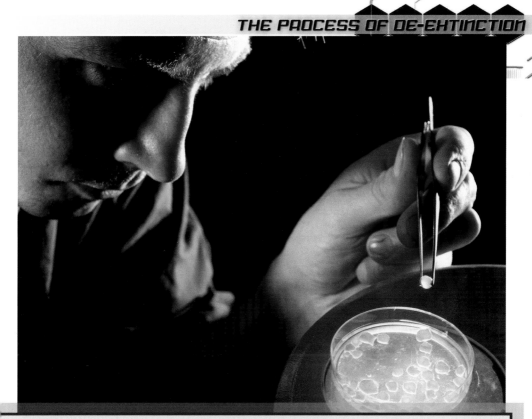

An embryologist performs in vitro fertilization (IVF). He removes egg-containing follicles from a petri dish. After fertilization by sperm, they will divide and be implanted into a surrogate's uterus.

the egg to divide and implant it into the elephant, where it would grow into a baby mammoth.

Second, rather than building mammoth DNA from scratch, scientists might start with elephant DNA. Elephant genes differ from mammoth genes at four hundred thousand locations. As many of these sections of DNA as possible would be altered to match mammoth genes. In addition, an elephant skin cell would be changed into an embryonic cell, and the altered DNA would be injected into the embryonic cell. The new embryonic cell would be stimulated to divide and then implanted into an elephant. The result, again, would be a new baby mammoth.

HOW CLOSE TO SUCCESS?

Cloning attempts are mostly conducted on endangered, rather than extinct, species, simply because it is much easier to obtain viable DNA from a living organism. The same techniques are used to clone extinct species, and both have been tried. Since the early 2000s, species that have been cloned include the guar (a wild ox), the banteng (a type of cow), the Pyrenean ibex (a wild goat), and the wild coyote. In nearly all cases, the clones died before birth or adulthood. They died for different reasons, but all had one thing in common—none were exact replicas of the parent. They were formed by combining the species' DNA with the DNA of a domesticated species, which then became the surrogate mother.

Clones often die from serious developmental abnormalities, possibly because the dividing cell contains a genome with adult chromosomes. In a normal embryo, dividing cells gradually differentiate into separate cell types—their genomes remain the same, but their epigenomes (the combination of genes that are expressed and unexpressed) change as the dividing cells become different adult cell types. If the original egg cell receives an adult nucleus (say, from a skin cell), it already has an adult epigenome, and the egg cell must reprogram it. Scientists do not understand exactly how this process works, but in clones, it often results in defects and death.

Some biologists hope cloning will help save endangered species. Ferris Jabr reported in *Scientific American* that, in 2009, two Brazilian organizations began saving blood and tissue samples from roadkill and other recently deceased animals. They hope eventually to use DNA from these samples to clone the animals and bolster dwindling populations. Meanwhile, they are using the DNA in a project to improve cloning techniques. Veterinarian Martha Gómez, of the

Audubon Center for the Research of Endangered Species in New Orleans, specializes in cloning various wild cats, using domestic cats as surrogate mothers. Gómez is hoping to simplify the cloning process.

But because of the expense, time required, and low success rate, many people do not see cloning as a reasonable method for saving endangered species. For every clone that lives, hundreds of egg cells and dozens of surrogate mothers are used. Furthermore, cloning does not address the main reasons animals become endangered— habitat loss and overhunting. An article by Philip Bethge in Spiegel Online quotes WWF wildlife expert Sybille Klenzendorf: "Habitats cannot be cloned." She says the large amount of money spent on cloning would be better spent to maintain habitats where the remaining animals can live and repopulate.

Cloning is difficult with living organisms and even more difficult with extinct species. Producing hybrids is more likely. According to Steven Novella, writing on the Neurologica Blog, Harvard geneticist George Church announced in February 2017 that his laboratory was about two years away from producing a mammoth hybrid by splicing mammoth genes into an Indian elephant. So far, they have spliced only forty-five pieces of mammoth DNA into elephant DNA. But as far as cloning an actual mammoth, Novella says, "we're not even close yet." Although all forms of de-extinction are possible, success is presumably some years away.

CHAPTER 3

EARLY EFFORTS AT DE-EXTINCTION

A 2017 article by Gerardo Ceballos and others in the *Proceedings of the National Academy of Sciences* (PNAS) warns that the sixth extinction, caused by human activity and ongoing in the twenty-first century, is much more serious than usually portrayed. The authors found that nearly a third of vertebrates—even those thought to have living populations—have lost 30 percent or more of their geographic ranges. More than 40 percent have lost 80 percent or more of their population sizes. The authors expect these declines to result in a cascade of losses in ecosystem functions and services on which people depend.

Plant species, too, are threatened by the mass extinction. In a 2010 study reported in DNews, 22 percent of four thousand species surveyed were classified as threatened, most by human-caused habitat loss. According to Stephen Hopper, director of the Royal Botanic Gardens in Kew, London, this plant study sets a baseline for future conservation efforts. Researchers from both the plant and animal studies emphasize the need to address the loss of organisms quickly. Conservation is one way to address extinction and endangered species. De-extinction, and use of similar techniques to produce more copies of endangered species, may be another.

Conservationists from the World Wildlife Fund (WWF) are de-horning rhinos to make them less vulnerable to poachers. They hope this will slow the loss of this highly endangered species.

LIKELY CANDIDATES FOR DE-EXTINCTION

So far, no animal species has successfully undergone de-extinction. But scientists are setting their sights on several species of recently lost animals for whom DNA is available. The woolly mammoth gets the most attention, but other probable candidates for de-extinction are the thylacine, passenger pigeon, and aurochs. Depending on the species, de-extinction methods will vary but possibly include

SAVING OLD-GROWTH REDWOODS

Earth's oldest and tallest trees are the coast redwoods, *Sequoia sempervirens*. These giants live for two to four thousand years. They grow 350 feet (107 m) high and more than 30 feet (9 m) across—the width of a house. They have lived on Earth for millions of years. But, in the mid-1800s, people began to cut them for lumber. By the 2010s, 96 percent of California's coast redwoods and 98 percent of all coast redwoods were gone.

According to Melissa Breyer in Treehugger.com, David Milarch, an arborist (a specialist in tree culture) has made it his life's work to save the coast redwood. He values this incredible tree for its beauty and history, its place in the coastal ecosystem, and its ability to store carbon—a key to combating climate change. Milarch founded the Archangel Ancient Tree Archive, a laboratory where arborists preserve and clone the genes of old-growth redwoods. When a redwood is cut or burned, it produces basal sprouts—new growth from its roots. Arborists harvested tissue from the basal sprouts of the twenty largest coast redwoods. In the laboratory, they cut these into very small pieces and use the process of micro-propagation, or tissue culture, to grow millions of tiny new redwood trees. They raise these clones to sapling size in the laboratory. Milarch's group is planting the saplings on the West Coast to replenish the cut forests. To ensure greater success as global warming continues, they are planting many saplings along the cool, foggy Oregon coast.

some type of reverse engineering by hybridization with related living species.

The thylacine, or Tasmanian tiger, is a carnivorous marsupial once found in Australia, Tasmania, and New Guinea. It went extinct in 1936 because of hunting and trapping by humans, who considered it a threat to the region's ill-fated sheep industry. Paleontologist Michael Archer and his colleagues have extracted thylacine DNA from the teeth, skin, and dried tissue of museum specimens. According to Archer (quoted by Brian Switek in *National Geographic*), the thylacine could either be cloned or successively hybridized with the closely related Tasmanian devil.

The Tasmanian tiger (thylacine), shown here in the Australian Museum, Sydney, could soon undergo de-extinction using DNA from museum specimens. But how will it fit into present-day ecosystems?

Martha, the last passenger pigeon, died in the Cincinnati Zoo in 1912. Passenger pigeon DNA is available from Martha and other museum specimens. Researchers think the best way to re-create the species is by reverse engineering from its closest living relative, the band-tailed pigeon. They would first sequence the genomes of both species and then tweak the DNA of the band-tailed pigeon, replacing regions where the two genomes differed with passenger pigeon DNA sequences.

Aurochs, wild cattle living in Europe and Asia, were the ancestors of today's domestic cattle. They went extinct in the early seventeenth century because of disease, habitat loss, and other factors. European scientists hope to reintroduce aurochs through the process of breeding back. They can use DNA sequencing to select primitive cattle breeds with DNA that produces cattle physically (and genetically) similar to aurochs. Eventually, they hope to return wild aurochs to the European landscape, but the project will take many years.

DNA SEQUENCING

Every living cell has a complete set of DNA, which is collected into chromosomes. Within a chromosome, DNA is divided into genes, each of which gives instructions for making a specific protein that controls some aspect of the organism's structure or function. Some DNA segments are regulatory; they turn genes on or off. Each nucleotide (basic unit) in DNA contains one of four bases (A, T, G, or C). The order of these bases along the DNA strand determines which protein will be formed.

DNA sequencing determines the exact order of bases along each gene. When all DNA on all chromosomes of an organism has been described, the organism's genome has been sequenced. The sequence tells scientists what genes are present, giving information on the organism's capabilities. Comparing genes of individuals or species and pinpointing differences can show which genes cause certain diseases, characteristics, or behaviors. In mammoth de-extinction, it shows which genes make mammoths different from elephants and which must be copied and spliced to further the process of de-extinction.

The peaks on this computer display show the sequence of nucleotide bases (A, T, C, and G) in a strand of DNA. DNA sequencing describes an organism's genetic code.

The quagga is a rare success story in the history of de-extinction. Quaggas went extinct in 1883. They were shot by South African farmers, who considered them competitors of grazing livestock. They were also killed for sport, game, and hides. Quaggas could not be cloned because the only DNA available is degraded. But quaggas were close relatives of the plains zebra. The two species look very much alike, except that the quagga had stripes only on its front half. In 1987, a South African taxidermist, Reinhold Rau, began a project to de-extinct the quagga by breeding back from the plains zebra. In 2016, the project was led by Eric Harley and Mike Gre-

ZOOLOGIE.

MAMMIFÈRES.   Chevaux.

1. LE CHEVAL.
2. LE COUAGGA.

This 1816 illustration from a French textbook shows a horse (*top*) and a quagga. The quagga may be relatively easy to de-extinct because of its similarity to the plains zebra.

gor of the University of Cape Town. It had produced five generations of animals, and six of one hundred offspring showed quagga coloration—that is, decreased striping and brown background color. But, although the new animals look like quaggas, researchers realize they likely have not reproduced all quagga characteristics and adaptations.

IMPLICATIONS OF DE-EXTINCTION

Dr. Beth Shapiro, from the University of California, Santa Cruz, is an expert in ancient DNA. Shapiro sees the de-extinction of extinct animals as both "exhilarating and terrifying," according to Elizabeth Quill in *Smithsonian Magazine*. She considers it a boon for scientific understanding and conservation but also fraught with ethical challenges. Species chosen for de-extinction, Shapiro feels, should inspire people to get excited about science and technology and have a positive effect on the environment. Her first choice is the mammoth, but she cautions that care would be needed to ensure that elephants, which are vital to the de-extinction process, would not be harmed. She also points out that mammoths resulting from de-extinction would not be clones, but hybrids. Researchers would use genetic engineering techniques to tweak elephant genomes, making their DNA sequences more mammothlike, rather than cloning from whole mammoth cell nuclei.

Shapiro also considers genetic manipulation valuable for preserving endangered species, for example, black and white rhinoceroses. As of 2015, only five white rhinos still existed anywhere in the world, and only one was male. This makes further reproduction of the species highly unlikely. Even if breeding occurred, the tiny population would result in excessive inbreeding. Genomes from cells of existing rhinos could be edited, replacing some genes with genes from skin or bone samples in museum collections. Edited cells inserted into remaining female rhinos could produce baby rhinos with different genomes and improve genetic diversity.

Thus, advances in biotechnology can be applied to research in both de-extinction and preservation of endangered species. Scientists disagree about the relative value of these approaches. Shapiro strongly believes in both. Joseph Bennett and his colleagues from the University of Ontario, Canada, do not. According to a paper described in Abigail Beall's article in the British newspaper the *Daily Mail*, Bennett feels that the cost of de-extinction uses money that could be better spent saving still-living, but endangered, species. The paper concludes, "It is unlikely that de-extinction could be justified on grounds of biodiversity conservation."

CHAPTER 4

PLANS FOR FUTURE DE-EXTINCTIONS

Besides the woolly mammoth, passenger pigeon, thylacine, aurochs, and quagga, scientists are considering other animals for possible de-extinction. Their list contains ten mammals and fourteen birds. Half became extinct in the twentieth century, but the other half includes some gone for several thousand years. Birds include the heath hen, dodo, Carolina parakeet, dusky seaside sparrow, Cuban macaw, ivory-billed woodpecker, imperial woodpecker, and the moa of New Zealand. Mammals include the Steller's sea cow, Caribbean monk seal, mastodon, and saber-toothed cat. DNA exists for most of these species in museum specimens, frozen carcasses, or other preserved material. How do scientists decide which animals to de-extinct?

GUIDELINES FOR DE-EXTINCTION

Save for the bucardo clone, which lived for only ten minutes, true de-extinction has not yet happened. But technological problems

The flightless moa, native to New Zealand, went extinct between 1300 and 1440 CE, due to overhunting. This moa specimen is in the Te Papa Museum in Wellington, New Zealand.

in any field are eventually overcome, and scientists expect that the processes involved in de-extinction will soon become routine. They are beginning to consider the implications of introducing revived species into the modern world.

Scientists have developed a set of four criteria for de-extinction, according to Gately and others, writing for the Debating Science blog of the University of Massachusetts Amherst. These criteria would allow de-extinction research to continue, while addressing the concerns of scientists who object to the process. The criteria are: 1) How easily can the species be brought back to life? This process depends on the availability of viable DNA and, if necessary, the ability to reconstruct the genome from close living relatives. 2) Can the conditions that caused the original extinction be prevented if the species is reintroduced into the wild? This criterion is particularly difficult for extinctions with obvious human causes, such as hunting or habitat loss. 3) Will the revived species have a place to live? Some scientists favor measures to protect and restore existing

TESTING THE CRITERIA: THE GASTRIC-BROODING FROG

Australia's gastric-brooding frog was discovered in the 1970s and became extinct by the 1980s. The female of this species reproduced by turning her stomach into a womb. She swallowed fertilized eggs, stopped eating and producing stomach acid, and raised the eggs inside her stomach. When they became young frogs, she vomited them up. As described by Gately and others in the Debating Science blog of the University of Massachusetts, Dr. Michael Archer, of the University of New South Wales, hopes to regenerate gastric-brooding frogs through cloning from frozen intact DNA. The frogs went extinct because of a fungal infection. A fungus-resistant gene inserted into the genome could prevent a second extinction. Because the extinction was recent, the frog's habitat still exists relatively unchanged. For these reasons, it is an excellent candidate for de-extinction.

habitat. A few (such as Dr. Michael Archer) think habitats should be created especially for regenerated species. 4) Will the regenerated species help or harm its new environment? Will it fit into the eco-system or become invasive?

CASE STUDY: WOOLLY MAMMOTH

Several laboratories around the world are working on woolly mammoth reconstruction. Scientists at the Ancient DNA Center of McMaster University have sequenced the DNA from the frozen soft tissue of two long-dead mammoths. The complete mammoth genome was published in 2015. According to Sarah Kaplan, writing in the *Washington Post*, the work provides "a gene-by-gene instruction manual on how to build a mammoth." Hendrik Poinar, one of the study's authors, explains that comparing differences in the mammoth genome and that of the Asian elephant shows what genetic changes made the mammoth what it was.

Dr. George Church, of Harvard University, working with the Long Now Foundation, is trying to make an Asian elephant with some mammoth characteristics. Church and his group are using genetic manipulation techniques to splice mammoth genes into the Asian elephant genome. A baby born from this altered genome would be an elephant-mammoth hybrid. In February 2017, Church announced that they had succeeded in splicing forty-five mammoth genes into elephant DNA and hope to have an elephant-mammoth hybrid embryo within two years. They are concentrating on inserting uniquely mammoth traits, such as hair, fat, and cold-adapted blood.

This image compares an African elephant (*left*) with the extinct woolly mammoth. The Asian elephant, which serves as a surrogate for mammoth de-extinction studies, is slightly smaller than either.

Church's embryo would be just a first step. Making a purely mammoth embryo would take many years. A major hurdle is that Asian elephants are endangered, and many people, including Church, think it would be unethical to use them as mammoth surrogates. Instead, they hope to use an artificial uterus to grow the babies to term in the laboratory. However, this technology did not exist as of 2017, and Church admits that, if it is not developed, he will be unable to resurrect the mammoth.

Even a mammoth-elephant hybrid could help repopulate the Siberian tundra, according to Russian scientist Sergey Zimov.

HOW TO EDIT DNA

The genetic manipulation used to insert, for example, mammoth DNA into elephant egg nuclei is based on a technique discovered in 2014. A molecular system that bacteria use to combat viruses, called CRISPR, can also be used to make precise changes in the DNA of other species. The bacterial genome is separated by spacers, or DNA segments of the viruses that previously attacked the bacteria. When the same virus attacks again, the bacterium makes a strand of RNA (similar to DNA), which attaches to the spacer. The invading virus attaches to the RNA at this point. The bacterium then cuts through both DNA and RNA, disabling and editing out the virus. Using CRISPR-like technology, scientists can cut and paste snippets of mammoth DNA into elephant cells, giving elephants woolly mammoth characteristics. CRISPR speeds up genome editing, by allowing many gene changes to be made at once.

This diagram illustrates CRISPR technology, including separation of DNA strands and building of RNA segments along them. In this way, mammoth genes can be inserted into elephant DNA.

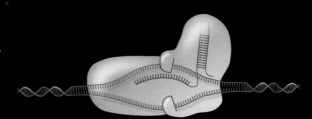

Sarah Kaplan, in the *Washington Post*, reports that, at a wildlife refuge called Pleistocene Park, Zimov hopes to reconstitute a pasture ecosystem common ten thousand years ago, with reindeer, bison, wolves, and mammoths. Mammoths were keystone species, instrumental in maintaining the pastureland. Zimov thinks reintroducing them would help revive it. This could prevent melting of the permafrost and slow global warming.

CASE STUDY: PASSENGER PIGEON

Flocks comprising hundreds of millions of passenger pigeons once darkened the skies of North America. In 2017, all that remained were 1,500 museum specimens. Since childhood, Ben Novak has dedicated himself to bringing the passenger pigeon back to life. Since 2013, Novak has worked on this project with Beth Shapiro and the Long Now Foundation at the Ancient DNA Laboratory, at the University of California, Santa Cruz. His plan for de-extinction of the passenger pigeon involves several steps: First, sequence the genomes of both the passenger pigeon and the band-tailed pigeon, its closest living relative. Second, insert fragments of passenger pigeon DNA into germ cells of the band-tailed pigeon, which will become eggs or sperm cells. Third, implant the altered DNA into egg cells of other pigeons, and over generations, develop new passenger pigeons that can produce their own offspring.

DNA remains in the cells of the museum birds' toe pads. However, it has become degraded and contaminated over the years. In the early 2000s, a new technique, called next-generation sequencing, made it possible to sequence even degraded passenger

Some museum specimens of passenger pigeons, such as this one, have viable DNA in their toe pads, which might be used in de-extinction attempts. Passenger pigeons went extinct in 1914.

pigeon DNA. New machines can analyze hundreds of thousands of short DNA fragments simultaneously. According to Steven Salzberg of Johns Hopkins University (quoted by Kelly Servick in a 2013 article in *Wired*), "In the past 10 years, sequencing has gotten approximately 500,000 times more efficient." By organizing segments of passenger pigeon DNA along the sequences of band-tailed pigeon DNA, scientists were able to determine the original order of DNA in the passenger pigeon genome.

By 2014, Novak and the other researchers had sequenced DNA from thirty-two specimens. All are very similar genetically—like cousins, Novak says. The group is working to sequence birds that are thousands of years old and compare them with newer birds. Determining the rate of change in the birds' genomes will help them understand the birds' ecology. This step would help ensure that regenerated birds could survive in nature. Many scientists do not think that this course of action is possible. Most of the pigeons' breeding and overwintering habitat has been destroyed, as has much of their major food source—beech nuts. Also, passenger pigeons apparently required extremely high population densities to survive. If only a few birds are introduced, they are likely to die out quickly. However, Novak remains optimistic. "I believe the passenger pigeon will survive because we have people committed to its survival," he says.

While many scientists are excited about the possibilities of de-extinction, Dave Strayer, a scientist with the Cary Institute for Ecosystem Studies, cautions that it may have serious ecological consequences. Strayer, writing in Liza Lester's blog for the Ecological Society of America, says that introducing a reconstituted species into an ecosystem is the equivalent of introducing an exotic species. Its effects may be positive or negative; but either way, they are impossible to predict or to control.

CHAPTER 5

THE ETHICS OF DE-EXTINCTION

In *Jurassic Park*, people undertook the de-extinction of dinosaurs because it was exciting and technologically challenging—and because it would make a lot of money. They forged ahead and figured out what they could do, but they never considered whether they *should* do it. They assumed they could handle anything that happened. They did not consider the ethics (much less the social or ecological consequences) of introducing extinct animals into the modern world. Some people think that this situation is exactly what is happening in the twenty-first century—not with dinosaurs, but with mammoths, passenger pigeons, thylacines, and others whose de-extinction is either occurring or being considered. Others think de-extinction is the only ethical thing to do.

THE PROS OF DE-EXTINCTION

According to Jamie Shreeve, writing in *National Geographic*, there are two basic arguments for de-extinction, or species revival. First, "we should do it because we can do it," and second, "we should do it because we have an *obligation* to do it." The "because we can" argument centers on scientific progress. The benefits of scientific discovery are never known until after the progress is made, the argument goes. Therefore, impeding that progress eliminates potential benefits. The "obligation" argument is a moral one—humans drove the species to extinction, so the least they can do is try to return the species to our world. That is, de-extinction would right the wrong humans caused by wiping out a species. But, Shreeve says, regardless of whether de-extinction advocates begin with a scientific or a moral argument, they usually end with a comment like, "it's just such a really cool idea."

One of de-extinction's strongest advocates is Stewart Brand. Brand is best known as the creator of the *Whole Earth Catalog*, first published in 1968. In 1996, he cofounded (with computer engineer Danny Hillis) the Long Now Foundation, a nonprofit concerned with long-term thinking. In a *National Geographic* article, Brand says the scientific reasons for undertaking de-extinction are the same reasons for protecting endangered species: preserving biodiversity, restoring ecosystems, and learning to prevent extinctions. But Brand's most compelling arguments relate to what he calls "the power of good news." He thinks the hope generated by de-extinction will strongly benefit conservation. The awe and wonder of seeing once-extinct animals come to life will, he hopes, arouse a passion for nature and conservation in new generations of children.

Brand sees de-extinction efforts as a great boon to conserving highly endangered species and ecosystems. Studying the genes of extinct species may help scientists determine why they became extinct. This knowledge can help save currently endangered species. In cases where the cause of extinction or near-extinction is known, that cause might be reversed. For example, the remaining Tasmanian devils have a facial cancer thought to be transmitted by a single gene.

The Long Now Foundation hopes to restore the genetic diversity of the endangered black-footed ferret by cryogenic artificial insemination (fertilizing live female ferrets with the frozen sperm of long-dead males).

Scientists could silence the gene causing this cancer in the lab, and return the immunized animals to the wild, where they would reproduce more quickly and soon replace those with the defective gene. This process would restore the population. Extinct species such as the mammoth and passenger pigeon were keystone species in their ecosystems. Restoring these species, Brand thinks, would help restore the lost ecosystems. This action could slow global warming and help restore biodiversity.

THE CONS OF DE-EXTINCTION

The Kimmela Center for Animal Advocacy lists four reasons to oppose de-extinction. First, the process ignores the welfare of the animals it supposedly regenerates, often treating them inhumanely. For example,

SAVING SEEDS TO PREVENT EXTINCTION

Lorraine Chow, writing for EcoWatch, reports that the sixth mass extinction is directly affecting the world's food crops. More than five thousand plant species are used as food (and thirty thousand more could be used), but only three species—corn, rice, and wheat—supply more than half of all plant calories consumed by humans. Crop species are threatened by extinction just as much as animals but are mostly ignored.

The Svalbard Global Seed Vault, on the island of Spitsbergen, Norway, was designed to protect the seeds of important food crops against any disaster, without human intervention. Since its opening in 2008, it has stored nearly a million packets of seeds. Like scientists trying to preserve or regenerate animals, the founders of the Global Seed Vault want to save plants by preserving their seeds. The Global Seed Vault is buried deep under a mountain north of the Arctic Circle. Its

The Svalbard Global Seed Vault was built into a mountainside under a deep layer of permafrost to protect it from climate change. Melting permafrost now endangers the vault.

builders assumed that, because it was buried in permafrost (frozen soil), the seeds would always be safe because permafrost would never melt, and the seeds would stay below freezing. But only eight years after the Global Seed Vault opened, Damian Carrington reported in *Wired* that record-high winter temperatures produced heavy rain instead of snow, and the Global Seed Vault entrance flooded. No seeds were damaged, but vault managers are now waterproofing the vault, and it is watched constantly. Like de-extinction, protection from extinction is a long-term project.

many elephant mothers and hundreds of eggs are used trying to create a single mammoth hybrid. Second, reviving a few species ignores the millions being lost in the current mass extinction. It uses valuable resources without stemming the tide of extinction. Third, de-extinction is not conservation. It preserves a small, not diverse component of the species' genetic blueprint but does not preserve or rebuild that species' genetic diversity or its ecosystem. Conservation biologist Kent Redford, quoted by Jason Koebler in *U.S. News & World Report*, says it may even destroy the ecosystem. He likens introducing newly regenerated species back into a changed ecosystem to introducing an exotic species, which could devastate other ecosystem members. Finally, de-extinction promotes the attitude that there is no need to worry about extinction because scientists can always bring extinct species back to life.

A strong voice against de-extinction is Stuart Pimm, a conservation ecologist from Duke University. In a 2013 *National Geographic* article, Pimm notes that de-extinction proponents want to resurrect "single, charismatic species," while ignoring the millions of plant, animal, and microbial species going extinct at alarming rates. The foods of these chosen species may be extinct, and even if not, returning them to their former habitats may be unsuccessful. For example, when the endangered Arabian oryx was returned to its habitat in Oman after a captive breeding program, the numbers of released captives quickly declined. (However, a program in the United Arab Emirates, where the animals are more protected, has been much more successful.) The bucardo, hunted to extinction in its native Pyrenees Mountains, would possibly suffer the same fate if returned. Unless the conditions that caused an extinction are corrected, that extinction would just occur again. For this and other reasons, Pimm considers de-extinction efforts a "colossal waste."

According to Pimm, politicians confronted with information on extinctions usually react in one of two ways. They suggest either

In 2009, after a captive breeding program, eight Arabian oryx were returned to their native desert habitat in the United Arab Emirates. By 2017, their numbers had grown to forty-three.

saving a very small remnant of the habitat or breeding the species in captivity (letting lab-coated scientists save the day). In either case, the response would prevent total extinction but still destroy the natural habitat. It would not preserve biodiversity, genetic diversity, or sustainable ecosystems. This response is the opposite of conservation, Pimm says, the real purpose of which is finding sustainable futures for natural systems. De-extinction efforts seduce funding agencies away from spending money on true conservation and toward a gimmicky, ultimately hopeless method. Shreeve states this objection succinctly: "Why waste resources trying to resurrect the dead when we can use them to save the sick?"

Legal experts also have questions, according to Virginia Gewin in *Discover*. In a 2013 conference at Stanford University, participants debated matters such as whether a resurrected species would be considered a genetically modified organism (GMO) or would be covered by the Endangered Species Act. If part of the DNA in the resurrected animal is original (as in DNA recovered from frozen mammoths), it becomes difficult to distinguish between extinct and endangered species. Stewart Brand suggests a new category: "exceptionally endangered" species, which are potentially recoverable. Chuck Bonham, director of the California Department of Fish and Wildlife, would like to see an agreement between regulators and scientists to work together on de-extinction and to make sure that, if de-extinction continues, preventing extinction also remains important.

ETHICS AND DE-EHTINCTION

Ben Minteer, writing for the Center for Humans and Nature, says many who champion de-extinction feel awe and wonder for human technology, rather than for the natural world. He considers Harvard

DE-EXTINCTION AND THE ENDANGERED SPECIES ACT

Dolly the sheep, born in 1996, was the first mammal cloned from an adult cell. Scientists soon saw cloning as a way to help repopulate endangered species, or even bring back extinct species. However, there is currently no legal framework that includes de-extinct species. The closest law is the Endangered Species Act. This act was designed to protect species that still exist by preventing destruction of their habitats or other actions that would threaten their populations. But the habitats of extinct species no longer exist. Many have not

existed for hundreds or thousands of years. De-extinct species might have no suitable place to live and reproduce. According to Dylan Novak, writing in the *North Carolina Journal of Law & Technology*, as the technologies of cloning and de-extinction advance, there is a growing need for a governing body to determine how to regulate the reintroduction of species returned from extinction.

Dolly the sheep, the first successfully cloned mammal, poses with Dr. Ian Wilmut at the Roslin Institute.

geneticist George Church to be one of these. Church considers regenerating birds such as the heath hen a "slam dunk." Minteer quotes Church as saying, "We can just make a few adjustments to the DNA … As an engineering project, birds are easy." Minteer contrasted this attitude with that of conservationist Aldo Leopold who, in 1938, worried about the effect of technology on the conservation ethic. "Our tools are better than we are, and grow faster than we do," Leopold said. "They suffice to crack the atom … But, they do not suffice for the oldest task in human history: to live on a piece of land without spoiling it."

De-extinction is a new field, and the ethical and legal controversies surrounding it may be just beginning. Minteer is concerned that extreme proponents of de-extinction, such as Stewart Brand and Stephen Kellert, professor emeritus of social ecology at Yale University, are overlooking an important factor. They incorrectly equate the bioengineered (regenerated) version of the organism with the original (now extinct) version. The two are not the same. Because of this difference, the bioengineered species is not adapted to the habitat in which it will be placed. Therefore, it will not have relationships with other species in the ecosystem, nor fit into the system. Although re-extinction of species may ease the guilt of some conservationists, Minteer says it fails as a conservation ethic and as a conservation strategy. It is just a curiosity. It is unlikely, in the long run, to have a major impact on biodiversity, conservation of vulnerable species, or protection of endangered habitats. It is exciting technology but poor conservation.

1883 The quagga goes extinct in South Africa.

1912 Martha, the last passenger pigeon, dies in the Cincinnati Zoo, making the species extinct.

1936 The last thylacine dies in Tasmania, making the species extinct.

1990 The novel *Jurassic Park*, by Michael Crichton, is published.

1996 Dolly the sheep is cloned; she is the first mammal cloned from an adult cell.

2003 On July 30, the only clone of Celia, the world's last bucardo (Pyrenean ibex) is born but dies after ten minutes.

2008 The Svalbard Global Seed Vault is opened, intending to preserve seeds of the world's crop plants under permafrost. Only eight years later (in 2016), the vault's entrance floods due to excessively warm winter temperatures.

2009 Two Brazilian organizations begin saving blood and tissue samples from recently deceased endangered species to use in cloning projects.

2010 A study is published by the Royal Botanic Gardens in London, analyzing four thousand species of plants threatened by habitat loss.

2013 In March, *National Geographic* publishes an entire issue devoted to de-extinction.
In May, Stanford University holds a conference devoted to laws and ethics related to de-extinction.

2014 The CRISPR technique, used in biotechnology to cut and paste DNA between species, is discovered.

2015 Genome sequencing of the woolly mammoth is completed.

2016 The quagga de-extinction project at Cape Town University has produced five generations of hybrids; six of the one hundred offspring have quagga characteristics.

2017 In February, George Church of Harvard University announces that his lab is within two years of producing a mammoth-elephant hybrid.
In May, an article on vertebrates facing extinction is published in the *Proceedings of the National Academy of Sciences*.

backcrossing Crossing a hybrid with one of its parents, or an organism with the same genetic characteristics as the parent, to obtain offspring more like that parent.

biotechnology Using biological processes to make technological or industrial products; for example, using genetic manipulation of microorganisms to produce antibiotics, hormones, and other products.

breeding back A form of artificial selection in which breeders begin with a modern species and selectively breed its members to obtain offspring with characters similar to an extinct ancestor.

cloning The process of making an exact replica of a biological unit (a piece of DNA, a cell, or an organism) by using the methods of biotechnology.

de-extinction Also called resurrection biology or species revivalism; the use of biotechnology techniques to return a species from extinction using saved cells of the species.

DNA Deoxyribonucleic acid, the molecule that forms chromosomes and contains genes; found in every cell of every living organism and containing the genetic information for making and reproducing that organism.

DNA sequencing Also called gene sequencing. The process of determining the precise order of the nucleotides, specifically the order of the four bases (A, T, G, and C) in the DNA molecule; allows identification of organisms and their genes and is the basis for genetic manipulation.

epigenome The combination of expressed and unexpressed genes in an organism's genome; that is, a genome contains all genes, but as the organism matures, some turn off and others turn on.

extinction The death of an entire species; the disappearance of a species of organism (including its specific DNA pattern) from life on Earth.

genetic engineering The process of altering genes to produce new characteristics in organisms; usually involves adding new gene segments to an organism's DNA or replacing existing gene segments with new ones assembled in a laboratory or taken from another organism.

genome The complete set of chromosomes (containing all genes with all DNA) in an organism; a genome is present in every cell and required to clone or otherwise reproduce the organism.

hybrid An organism produced by breeding two organisms of different species (for example, a mammoth and an elephant).

hybrid vigor Superior growth, health, disease resistance, and other characteristics often displayed by crossbred (hybrid) organisms.

in vitro fertilization (IVF) A reproductive technique in which an egg is fertilized by a sperm outside the body (for example, in a test tube) and later implanted into the uterus of a female.

mass extinction The extinction of a very large number of species over a relatively short geological time period, probably due to a catastrophic event such as a meteor strike or very rapid climate change. Scientists know of five mass extinctions and a sixth is underway.

parthenogenesis A form of reproduction occurring in some plants, insects, fish, and reptiles in which an unfertilized egg spontaneously develops into a new organism.

reverse engineering Reproducing one item by studying and re-creating the composition of another, similar, item; in de-extinction, reproducing an extinct species by starting with a related species and tweaking its genome until it closely matches the extinct species.

stem cells Undifferentiated cells that can transform into any type of cell; during development, most differentiate into specific cell types (brain, muscle, etc.). They can also divide by mitosis to produce more stem cells.

surrogate mother A female that becomes pregnant by in vitro fertilization and implantation of an embryo from another source and who carries the embryo to term; used in cloning.

Alliance for Humane
  Biotechnology (AHB)
155 21st Avenue
San Francisco, CA 94121
(415) 386-8414
Website: www.humanebiotech.org
AHB hopes to raise public aware-
  ness of the social implications
  of genetic engineering and
  reproductive technologies.
  The website includes a short
  course (AHB 101) that gives
  a time line of biotechnology,
  information on patents, a
  brief discussion on genetic
  determinism, and a discussion
  of bioethics.

Alliance for Zero Extinction (AZE)
c/o American Bird Conservancy
1731 Connecticut Avenue NW,
  3rd Floor
Washington, DC 20009
(888) 247-3624
Website: www.zeroextinction.org
  /index.html
AZE is an alliance of eighty-
  eight worldwide biodiversity
  organizations and is dedicated to preventing extinction
  by safeguarding the environments of critically endangered species now limited to

single locations. The website
  provides a live map, FAQs,
  and other information.

Canadian Coalition for Genetic
  Fairness
151 Frederick Street, Suite 400
Kitchener, ON N2H 2M2
Canada
(800) 998-7398
Website: http://ccgf-cceg.ca/en
  /home
Facebook:@FightingGenetic
  Discrimination
Instagram and Twitter:
  @GeneticFairness
This organization is human orient-
  ed; it is dedicated to preventing
  genetic discrimination among
  Canadians. The website in-
  cludes short, simple answers
  to questions about genes and
  genetic discrimination.

Council for Responsible Genetics
5 Upland Road, Suite 3
Cambridge, MA 02140
(617) 868-0870
Website: www.councilfor
  responsiblegenetics.org
Facebook: @GeneWatch
Instagram and Twitter: @CRG_
  Genewatch

This group is dedicated to serving the public interest and fostering public debate about social, ethical, and environmental aspects of genetics and biotechnology. The website includes many links to articles on related topics.

Defenders of Wildlife
1130 17th Street NW
Washington, DC 20036
(800) 385-9712
Website: www.defenders.org
Facebook: @DefendersofWildlife
Instagram and Twitter:
    @Defenders
Defenders of Wildlife protects endangered species and habitat by action in politics, in the courts, and in the field. The website provides photos and information on animals and habitats, as well as on the organization's projects.

Genome Canada
150 Metcalfe Street, Suite 2100
Ottawa, ON K2P 1P1
Canada
(613) 751-4474
Website: www.genomecanada.ca
Facebook, Instagram, and Twitter:

@GenomeCanada
This nonprofit organization is funded by the Canadian government. Its members help people and organizations develop new ideas for the use of genomics by providing funding and moving information across various sectors, including health, agriculture, and the environment. The website answers simple questions about genomics and describes the organization's programs.

Human Cloning Foundation
c/o B. Hennenfent
PO Box 375
Roseville, IL 61473
(571) 422-9750
Website: www.humancloning.org
Instagram and Twitter:
    @humancloning
This nonprofit organization supports human cloning technology, stem cell research, and infertility treatments to cure health and fertility problems and to prolong life. The website includes considerable information on reasons for human cloning and myths about cloning.

International Fund for Animal
Welfare (IFAW)
290 Summer Street
Yarmouth Port, MA 02675
(800) 932-4329
Website: www.ifaw.org
/united-states
Facebook: @ifaw
Instagram and Twitter:
@action4ifaw
IFAW is an international organization for wildlife protection and conservation. They protect animal populations and environments, prevent wildlife crime, and rescue animals. The website includes fact sheets on animals and current projects.

The Long Now Foundation
2 Marina Boulevard
Fort Mason Center Building A
San Francisco, CA 94123
(415) 561-6297
Website: http://longnow.org
Facebook, Instagram, and Twitter:
@longnow
This organization is dedicated to very long-term thinking and training people to think about the future. The Revive & Restore Project deals with "genetic rescue of endangered and extinct species." The FAQ, Blog, and Get Involved tabs provide information on the project.

US Food and Drug
Administration (FDA)
Animal Cloning Section
10903 New Hampshire Avenue
Silver Spring, MD 20993
(888) 463-6332
Website: https://www.fda.gov
/AnimalVeterinary
/SafetyHealth
/AnimalCloning/default.htm
Facebook: @FDA
Instagram and Twitter:
@US_FDA
This part of the US government gives general information on animal cloning and specific information on projects being carried out in the United States. The information is mostly related to food safety and includes a primer on cloning and myths about cloning.

Anders, Mason. *DNA, Genes, and Chromosomes.* North Mankato, MN: Capstone Press, 2018.

Bond, Dave. *Genetic Engineering* (STEM: Shaping the Future). Broomall, PA: Mason Crest, 2017.

Burgan, Michael. *Genetic Engineering: Science, Technology, Engineering.* New York, NY: Children's Press, 2016.

Henneberg, Susan. *Genetic Engineering* (Current Controversies). New York, NY: Greenhaven Publishing, 2017.

Hirsch, Rebecca E. *De-Extinction: The Science of Bringing Lost Species Back to Life.* Minneapolis, MN: Twenty-First Century Books, Lerner Publishing Group, 2017.

Kolbert, Elizabeth. *The Sixth Extinction: An Unnatural History.* Reprint ed. New York, NY: Picador, Henry Holt and Company, 2015.

Lachner, Elizabeth. *Bioengineering* (The Biotechnology Revolution). New York, NY: Britannica Educational Publishing, 2016.

Langwith, Jacqueline. *Cloning* (Opposing Viewpoints). Farmington Hills, MI: Greenhaven Press, 2012.

Mezrich, Ben. *Woolly: The True Story of the Quest to Revive One of History's Most Iconic Creatures.* New York, NY: Atria Books, 2017.

Rhodes, Wendell. *Threatened, Endangered, and Extinct Species* (Spotlight on Ecology and Life Science). New York, NY: Rosen Publishing, 2017.

Rogers, Kara, ed. *Cloning* (The Biotechnology Revolution). New York, NY: Britannica Educational Publishing, 2016.

Shapiro, Beth. *How to Clone a Mammoth.* Princeton, NJ: Princeton University Press, 2015.

BIBLIOGRAPHY

Arnold, Carrie. "Virgin Birth in Animals: Parthenogenesis Is No Miracle in Animal Kingdom." HuffPost, December 27, 2012. http://www.huffingtonpost.com/2012/12/27/virgin-birth-in-animals-parthenogenesis_n_2372246.html.

Beall, Abigail. "Is Bringing Extinct Animals Back to Life Worth It? Reviving Old Species Will Cause Many of Earth's Existing Animals to Die Out." DailyMail.com, February 28, 2017. http://www.dailymail.co.uk/sciencetech/article-4257542/De-extinction-cause-existing-animals-die-out.html.

Bethge, Philip. "Scientists Hope Cloning Will Save Endangered Animals." Spiegel Online, November 8, 2012. http://www.spiegel.de/international/world/scientists-hope-interspecies-cloning-will-save-endangered-animals-a-865932.html.

Biello, David. "Ancient DNA Could Return Passenger Pigeons to the Sky." *Scientific American*, August 29, 2014. https://www.scientificamerican.com/article/ancient-dna-could-return-passenger-pigeons-to-the-sky.

Brand, Stewart. "The Case for Reviving Extinct Species." *National Geographic*, March 12, 2013. http://news.nationalgeographic.com/news/2013/03/130311-deextinction-reviving-extinct-species-opinion-animals-science.

Breyer, Melissa. "This Man Is Cloning Old-Growth Redwoods and Planting Them in Safe Places (video)." Treehugger, March 8, 2017. https://www.treehugger.com/natural-sciences/man-cloning-old-growth-redwoods-and-planting-them-safe-places-video.html.

Carrington, Damian. "The Arctic Doomsday Seed Vault Flooded. Thanks, Global Warming." *Wired*, May 19, 2017. https://www.wired.com/2017/05/arctic-doomsday-seed-vault-flooded-thanks-global-warming.

Ceballos, Gerardo, Paul R. Ehrlich, and Rodolfo Dirzo. "Biological Annihilation via the Ongoing Sixth Mass Extinction Signaled by Vertebrate Population Losses and Declines." *Proceedings of the National Academy of Sciences*, May 23, 2017. http://www.pnas.org/content/114/30/E6089.full.

Chow, Lorraine. "Global Food Crops Also Face Earth's Sixth Great Mass Extinction." EcoWatch, September 26, 2017. https://www.ecowatch.com/food-mass-extinction-2489790982.html?utm_campaign=RebelMouse&utm_medium=social&utm_source=facebook&utm_content=EcoWatch.

Crichton, Michael. *Jurassic Park.* New York, NY: Alfred A. Knopf, 2009.

DNews. "20 Percent of Plant Species Face Extinction." Seeker, September 29, 2010. https://www.seeker.com/20-percent-of-plant-species-face-extinction-1765116350.html.

Futurism Staff. "Best Clone Movies." Retrieved September 21, 2017. https://futurism.media/best-clone-movies.

Gately, Bethany, Mark Pastore, and Mark Salhany. "De-extinction: Guidelines for Species Revival." Debating Science Blog, College of Natural Sciences, University of Massachusetts Amherst, December 5, 2013. http://blogs.umass.edu/natsci397a-eross/de-extinction-guidelines-for-species-revival-2.

Gewin, Virginia. "Laws Lag Behind Science in De-Extinction Debate." *Discover: The Crux*, June 5, 2013. http://blogs.discovermagazine.com/crux/2013/06/05/laws-lag-behind-science-in-de-extinction-debate/#.WYNfCbpFw2w.

Ghosh, Pallab. "Mammoth Genome Sequence Completed." BBC News, April 23, 2015. http://www.bbc.com/news/science-environment-32432693.

Human Cloning Foundation. "Books about Human Cloning (Fiction) Reviewed by a Member of the Human Cloning Foundation." Retrieved September 21, 2017. http://www.humancloning.org/fiction.htm.

Jabr, Ferris. "Will Cloning Ever Save Endangered Animals?" *Scientific American*, March 11, 2013. https://www.scientificamerican.com/article/cloning-endangered-animals.

Kaplan, Sarah. "'De-Extinction' of the Woolly Mammoth: A Step Closer." *Washington Post*, April 24, 2015. https://www.washingtonpost

.com/news/morning-mix/wp/2015/04/24/de-extinction-and-the
-wooly-mammoth-genome/?utm_term=.4f1be06b5d67.

Kimmela Center for Animal Advocacy, Inc. "Four Reasons Why We
Should Oppose 'De-Extinction'." April 4, 2013. http://www
.kimmela.org/2013/04/04/four-reasons-why-we-should-oppose
-de-extinction.

Lester, Liza. "De-Extinction, a Risky Ecological Experiment." Ecological Society of America, February 18, 2016. http://www.esa.org
/esablog/guest-posts/de-extinction-a-risky-ecological-experiment.

Minteer, Ben A. "The Perils of De-Extinction." *Minding Nature* 8(1),
Center for Humans and Nature, January 2015. https://www
.humansandnature.org/the-perils-of-de-extinction.

Novak, Dylan. "De-Extinction and the Endangered Species Act." *North
Carolina Journal of Law and Technology*, March 20, 2013. http://
ncjolt.org/de-extinction-and-the-endangered-species-act.

Novella, Steven. "De-Extinction." Neurologica Blog, February 28, 2017.
http://theness.com/neurologicablog/index.php/de-extinction.

Pimm, Stuart. "Opinion: The Case Against Species Revival." *National
Geographic*, March 12, 2013. http://news.nationalgeographic.com
/news/2013/03/130312--deextinction-conservation-animals
-science-extinction-biodiversity-habitat-environment.

Quill, Elizabeth. "These Are the Extinct Animals We Can, and Should,
Resurrect." *Smithsonian Magazine*, May 2015. http://www
.smithsonianmag.com/science-nature/these-are-extinct-animals
-we-can-should-resurrect-180954955.

Sarchet, Penny. "Can We Grow Woolly Mammoths in the Lab? George
Church Hopes So." *New Scientist*, February 16, 2017. https://www
.newscientist.com/article/2121503-can-we-grow-woolly
-mammoths-in-the-lab-george-church-hopes-so.

Servick, Kelly. "The Plan to Bring the Iconic Passenger Pigeon Back
from Extinction." *Wired*, March 15, 2013. https://www.wired
.com/2013/03/passenger-pigeon-de-extinction.

Shreeve, Jamie. "Species Revival: Should We Bring Back Extinct Species?" *National Geographic*, March 6, 2013. http://news.nationalgeographic .com/news/2013/03/130305-science-animals-extinct-species-revival -deextinction-debate-tedx.

Switek, Brian. "How to Resurrect Lost Species." *National Geographic*, March 19, 2013. http://news.nationalgeographic.com/news /2013/13/130310-extinct-species-cloning-deextinction-genetics -science.

Switek, Brian. "Reinventing the Mammoth." *National Geographic*, March 19, 2013. http://phenomena.nationalgeographic .com/2013/03/19/reinventing-the-mammoth.

Welsh, Jennifer. "These Are the 24 Animals Scientists Want to Bring Back from Extinction." *Business Insider*, March 4, 2014. http:// www.businessinsider.com/animals-for-de-extinction-2014-3?op=1.

Winstead, Edward R. "In South Africa, the Quagga Project Breeds Success." Genome News Network (GNN), October 20, 2000. http:// www.genomenewsnetwork.org/articles/10_00/Quagga_project.shtml.

Zimmer, Carl. "Bringing them Back to Life." *National Geographic*, April 2013. http://www.nationalgeographic.com/magazine/2013 /04/species-revival-bringing-back-extinct-animals.

Zutter, Natalie. "The Theme of *Orphan Black*'s Final Season Is Protest." Tor.com, June 12, 2017. https://www.tor.com/2017/06/12/orphan -black-season-5-the-few-who-dare-television-review.

INDEX

ABOUT THE AUTHOR

Carol Hand has a PhD in zoology, with a specialization in ecology and environmental sciences. She has taught college biology, worked for standardized-testing companies, developed multimedia science and technology curricula (including titles on life science, the environment, and genetics), and written numerous science and technology books for young people. She has a strong interest in protecting endangered species and in methods for preserving them.

PHOTO CREDITS

Cover, p. 1 Patrick Aventurier/Gamma-Rapho/Getty Images; pp. 4, 7, 15, 24, 32, 41 NikoNomad/Shutterstock.com; p. 6 Photo 12/Alamy Stock Photo; p. 8 Simon Littlejohn/NIS/Minden Pictures/Getty Images; p. 9 Leonardo Candamo/LUZPhoto/Redux; p. 12 AF archive/Alamy Stock Photo; p. 16 Daniel Eskridge/Stocktrek Images/Getty Images; p. 17 Kazuhiro Nogi/AFP/Getty Images; p. 18 BSIP/Universal Images Group/Getty Images; p. 21 Geoff Tompkinson/Science Source; p. 25 Desmond Kwande/AFP/Getty Images; p. 27 Torsten Blackwood/AFP/Getty Images; p. 29 Alfred Pasieka/Science Photo Library/Getty Images; p. 30 Florilegius/SSPL/Getty Images; p. 33 Marty Melville/AFP/Getty Images; p. 36 Walter Meyers/Science Source; p. 37 Monica Schroeder/Science Source; p. 39 Gary G Gibson/Science Source/Getty Images; p. 43 John E. Marriott/All Canada Photos/Getty Images; p. 44 Arterra/Universal Images Group/Getty Images; p. 46 Karim Sahib/AFP/Getty Images; p. 48 Robert Wallis/Corbis Historical/Getty Images; back cover and interior pages (circular element), interior pages (grid and circuit board patterns) Titima Ongkantong/Shutterstock.com.

Design: Nelson Sá; Layout: Tahara Anderson; Senior Editor: Kathy Kuhtz Campbell; Photo Researcher: Nicole Baker